Extreme Sports No Limits!

Extreme Wakeboarding

Bobbie Kalman

Crabtree Publishing Company

www.crabtreebooks.com

Created by Bobbie Kalman

Dedicated by Lisa Ariganello
For my mom, Robin, and for Dennis as you embark on an exciting future together

Editor-in-Chief
Bobbie Kalman

Writing team
Bobbie Kalman
Kylie Burns

Substantive editor
Kelley MacAulay

Editors
Molly Aloian
Rebecca Sjonger
Kathryn Smithyman

Design
Katherine Kantor

Production coordinator
Heather Fitzpatrick

Photo research
Crystal Foxton

Consultant
Raydon McCrea, member, Ontario Water Ski Association

Special thanks to
Hyperlite Wakeboards, Lu Le and Orlando Watersports Complex

Illustrations
Katherine Kantor: pages 10, 11, 15, 22-23
Bonna Rouse: pages 9, 12-13

Photographs
© Larry Beard/Acclaim Stock Photography: page 13
© Rick Doyle/CORBIS: page 6
Hyperlite Wakeboards: back cover, pages 4, 7, 8-9, 10, 11, 16, 17, 21, 24, 27, 28, 30
Mike Isler/Icon SMI: pages 18-19, 20, 25, 26, 29
Lu Le: pages 14, 31
Other images by Corbis

Crabtree Publishing Company

www.crabtreebooks.com   1-800-387-7650

Copyright © **2006 CRABTREE PUBLISHING COMPANY.**
All rights reserved. No part of this publication may be
reproduced, stored in a retrieval system or be transmitted in
any form or by any means, electronic, mechanical, photocopying,
recording, or otherwise, without the prior written permission
of Crabtree Publishing Company. In Canada: We acknowledge
the financial support of the Government of Canada through the
Book Publishing Industry Development Program (BPIDP) for our
publishing activities.

Cataloging-in-Publication Data
Kalman, Bobbie.
   Extreme wakeboarding / Bobbie Kalman.
      p. cm. -- (Extreme sports no limits!)
   Includes index.
   ISBN-13: 978-0-7787-1680-8 (rlb)
   ISBN-10: 0-7787-1680-5 (rlb)
   ISBN-13: 978-0-7787-1726-3 (pbk)
   ISBN-10: 0-7787-1726-7 (pbk)
   1. Wakeboarding--Juvenile literature. 2. Extreme sports--Juvenile literature.
I. Title. II. Series.
   GV840.W34K34 2006
   797.3'2--dc22
                                                      2005035788
                                                             LC

**Published in
the United States**

PMB16A
350 Fifth Ave.
Suite 3308
New York, NY
10118

**Published
in Canada**

616 Welland Ave.
St. Catharines, Ontario
Canada
L2M 5V6

**Published in the
United Kingdom**

White Cross Mills
High Town, Lancaster
LA1 4XS
United Kingdom

**Published
in Australia**

386 Mt. Alexander Rd.
Ascot Vale (Melbourne)
VIC 3032

CONTENTS

WAKE UP TO WAKEBOARDING

Wakeboarding is one of the newest and fastest-growing watersports in the world. A wakeboarder rides a small board called a **wakeboard** while holding a **tow rope**. The tow rope is attached to a **powerboat**. The boat creates a **wake**, or a series of small V-shaped waves. The wakeboarder jumps over the wake to perform amazing **tricks**, or moves. Wakeboarding takes place mainly on small bodies of water, such as lakes and rivers.

An extreme wakeboarder needs to have experience, skill, great balance, and, of course, no fear!

ARE YOU AWAKE?

Wakeboarding is an **extreme sport**. In extreme sports, athletes challenge themselves to push the limits of their sports. For many riders, wakeboarding is a fun way to spend time on the water. For **professional** or "pro" wakeboarders, it's a way of life! Pro riders make a living by competing in wakeboarding competitions. They are constantly working to create more daring and difficult tricks.

GET CULTURED!

Wakeboarding is a sport that has its own **culture**. A culture is a set of values that a group of people share. Wakeboarding culture includes its own style of music and clothing, as well as its own **lingo**, or language. Some of the most famous wakeboarding pros have their own brands of wakeboards, **bindings**, and clothing. There are even wakeboarding video games and computer games that allow kids who live far from water to experience the thrill of wakeboarding in their own homes!

EXTREME DANGER!

As you read this book, keep in mind that professional wakeboarders train for years to master their sport. Do not attempt anything shown in this book!

CATCH THE WAVE

*The Skurfer looked similar to a **snowboard**, and as a result, many of the early wakeboard tricks were actually snowboarding moves performed on water! The image above shows Tony Finn riding a Skurfer in 1987.*

Wakeboarding was developed by surfers who rode their **surfboards** in the wakes of powerboats. Surfboards were designed to be used on big ocean waves, however. The large surfboards were difficult to control on small wakes. This problem was solved in 1985, when an American surfer named Tony Finn created the **Skurfer**. The Skurfer was a smaller version of a surfboard. The new board was perfect for performing **surface tricks** on small waves. Surface tricks are performed on water, not in the air.

SKURFER DUDE!

The Skurfer was popular, but it was difficult to use. For example, riders had trouble climbing onto the board when it was in the water. If riders fell off in deep water, they often struggled to get back on their boards! The Skurfer was also narrower than a surfboard, so balancing on it was tricky.

THE NEW WAVE

Wakeboarding really took off in 1990, when Herb O'Brien invented the **Hyperlite**. The Hyperlite was a new board that improved upon the Skurfer's design. It had **neutral buoyancy**, which meant the board could float on the surface of water, but it could also be pulled under water. Neutral buoyancy allowed riders to get back on their boards easily after falls. The Hyperlite also had thin edges that allowed the board to cut across the water in quick, short turns.

*Skilled wakeboarders could perform impressive **aerial tricks** on Hyperlite boards. Aerial tricks are moves performed in the air.*

TIMELINE

1985: Tony Finn adds bindings to the Skurfer when Mike and Mark Pascoe give him the idea based on their windsurfing experiences.

1987: Finn publishes the first wakeboard instruction manual, called The Skurfer's Guide to Water Ski Boarding.

1989: Jimmy Redmon creates the World Wakeboard Association (WWA).

1990: The first-ever Skurfer championship competition is televised; Herb O'Brien designs and builds the Hyperlite wakeboard.

1991: The World Sports & Marketing company is created to plan and promote extreme water-sports events, including the Pro Wakeboard Tour.

1992: The first pro-wakeboarding events are held in the U.S.A.

1993: The first wakeboarding magazine is launched; Redmon creates a **twin-tip wakeboard**.

1995: For the first time, European riders compete in the World Wakeboard Championship.

1996: Millions of television viewers watch the first **X Games** wakeboarding competition.

1998: The Vans Triple Crown of Wakeboarding and the Wakeboard World Cup competitions begin.

1999: Wakeboarding events are included in the first Gravity Games competitions.

2000: Pro-wakeboarding competitions are permitted to include **obstacles**.

BOARD BASICS

In the past, wakeboarders rode either **single-tip** wakeboards or twin-tip wakeboards. A single-tip board is rounded at one end and square at the other end. Only the rounded end of the board can move forward through the water. A twin-tip board is rounded at both ends. It can move forward from either end. Today, almost all wakeboarders ride twin-tip boards.

TAKE YOUR POSITION

A wakeboarder usually rides his or her board in either **regular stance** or **goofy stance**. In regular stance, the wakeboarder rides with his or her right foot forward. In goofy stance, the wakeboarder rides with his or her left foot forward.

SWITCHING THINGS UP

Twin-tip boards are more popular than single-tip boards because wakeboarders can ride them **switchstance**. To ride switchstance, a wakeboarder who usually rides in one stance, switches to the other stance. For example, a rider who is wakeboarding on a twin-tip board in regular stance, can turn his or her upper body around to face the other way and begin riding in goofy stance.

TWIN-TIP WAKEBOARD

*The front end of a board is called the **nose**.*

*The edges of the board are called **rails**.*

*Many wakeboards have **fins** built into the front and back ends of the board. Fins help the rider steer the board. Most boards have two fins, one at the nose and one at the tail, but some wakeboards have as many as six fins. Some boards also come with removable fins that can be added to the bottom of the boards.*

*The **toeside** of a board is the side the rider's toes face. The **heelside** of a board is the side the rider's heels face.*

*Wakeboards are made of durable materials, such as **polyurethane**, **fiberglass**, and **graphite**. Polyurethane is a type of foam. It is used to make a board's inner **core**, or center. The core is then wrapped in fiberglass. Expensive, high-quality boards are wrapped in a combination of fiberglass and graphite, making them incredibly strong. These boards are also lightweight, so they are easier for riders to maneuver.*

*The back end of a board is called the **tail**.*

ROCKIN' WAKEBOARDS!

The bottom of a wakeboard is curved. This curve is called the wakeboard's **rocker**. There are two main types of rockers: **continuous** and **three-stage**. A wakeboard with continuous rocker has an uninterrupted curve from end to end. A wakeboard with three-stage rocker is flat in the middle and curves up at each end, as a skateboard does.

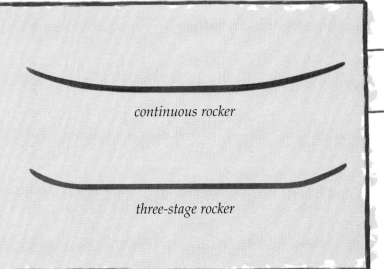

continuous rocker

three-stage rocker

PUT IT IN GEAR

Like many sports, wakeboarding can be risky, so it's important that athletes wear protective gear to stay safe. Extreme wakeboarders use high-quality gear to prevent injuries on the water.

TOW THE LINE

Without a tow rope, wakeboarding wouldn't exist! The tow rope is usually 60 to 70 feet (18-21 m) long. It is made of materials that do not stretch easily. Materials that are too stretchy could cause riders to spring backward or be yanked forward if the powerboat begins moving too quickly.

SELF-PRESERVATION

The most important pieces of equipment for athletes taking part in watersports are **personal floatation devices** (PFDs), or life vests. PFDs are vests that riders wear to stay afloat in water. These vests are lightweight and come in several styles. They are made of stretchy material that provides a snug fit and allows maximum flexibility.

HARD HELMETS

Helmets offer riders protection from possible head injuries. Helmets have hard plastic shells that protect riders during **wipeouts**, or falls. Most competitions require riders to wear helmets.

THE WETSUIT

Being in cold water can quickly lower a rider's body temperature. Many wakeboarders wear body-hugging **wetsuits** when they perform their sport in cold waters. Wetsuits are made of stretchy materials that hold in a rider's body heat. When wakeboarders ride in warm waters, however, they may prefer to wear bathing suits.

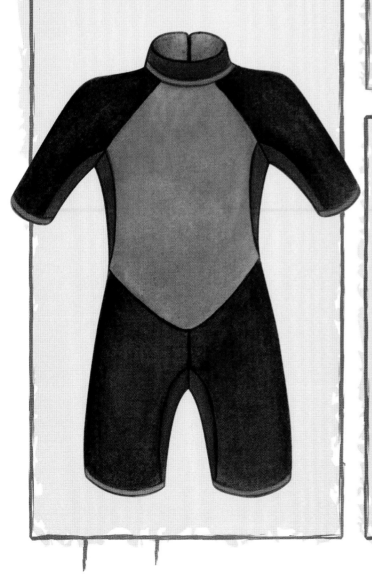

BINDERS, KEEPERS!

Bindings are gear made from a heavy foam material that hold a rider's feet in place on a wakeboard. Bindings are placed shoulder-width apart in the middle of the wakeboard. They make it possible for riders to perform daring turns and tricks.

CAN YOU HANDLE IT?

The **handles** used on tow ropes are usually 13 to 15 inches (33-38 cm) wide. Many handles have second **grips** located below the handles. A rider uses the grip when performing a **handle pass** behind his or her back. If the rider is twisting his or her body around, it is easier to do so while holding the small grip, rather than the larger handle.

grip ——

THE NEED FOR SPEED

Extreme wakeboarders perform their sport on the wakes created by powerboats. To create enough waves for a rider, a powerboat must reach speeds of at least 20 miles per hour (32 kph). Some boats are designed specifically for use in pro-wakeboarding competitions. These boats have **towers**, **board racks**, and **ballast tanks**. For most **recreational** wakeboarders, however, any powerboat will do!

A tower is a frame that extends up and across the front end of a powerboat. A rider's tow rope is attached to the tower. Attaching the tow rope to a high location such as the tower allows the rider to perform aerial tricks.

Board racks on the tower hold wakeboards that are not in use.

The driver must be very familiar with the boat, waterway, rider, and competition course. The driver should have experience driving a boat and towing a rider.

GETTING PERSONAL

Personal watercrafts (PWCs) are sometimes used in recreational wakeboarding. PWCs can travel on small waterways where larger boats do not fit. Some PWCs are made with special parts to which tow ropes can be attached. For many riders, a PWC is an affordable way to enjoy wakeboarding.

The **spotter** is a person in the boat who watches the wakeboarder closely. The spotter has a big responsibility. He or she must watch the rider and relay all the wakeboarder's **hand signals** (see page 21) to the driver. If there is a problem, the spotter alerts the driver immediately.

As the boat speeds along, ballast tanks at the back fill with water. These tanks help weigh down the back of the boat and create an enormous wake.

CATCHING A WAKE

At the beginning of a wakeboarding ride, the rider floats in the water, as shown right. The rider is positioned with the board on its side. The board is partially under water. When the rider is ready, he or she yells a phrase such as "Let 'er rip!" to let the driver know that it's okay to take off!

ON YOUR FEET!

The driver **accelerates**, or speeds up, gradually to 20 miles per hour (32 kph). As the driver accelerates, the force of the water pushes the wakeboard up to the water's surface, as shown right. The rider stands up as the wakeboard rises and pulls the tow rope toward the side of his or her body that will face forward.

MAY I CUT IN?

Once the rider is standing, he or she steers the wakeboard into the **flats**. The flats are calm areas of water on either side of a wake. Once the rider is in the flats, he or she **cuts into a wake**. To cut into a wake, the rider uses the sides of the board to steer it toward the wave. Pressing on different sides of the board moves the board in different directions. For example, if a rider is standing with his or her toes facing the left side of the board, then the left side of the board is the toeside, and the right side of the board is the heelside. To move toward a wake on the left, the rider cuts in on the toeside by shifting his or her body weight onto his or her toes. This movement presses the left edge of the board into the water, causing the board to turn left into the wake. A wakeboarder cutting in on the toeside is shown below.

5. The rider performs a trick in the air.

1. First, the rider stands up on the wakeboard behind the boat. The rider is in the center of the wake.

4. The rider hits the wake and flies into the air.

3. The rider presses the toeside of the board into the water to move the board toward the wake.

2. The rider steers the wakeboard into the flats.

TRICKS OF THE TRADE

Grabs! Spins! Flips! These sound like words used to describe a thrilling roller-coaster ride. In fact, these are just some of the basic tricks performed by wakeboarders. Wakeboarding tricks are all about **getting air**, or flying up into the air. Once a rider masters these tricks, he or she will be able to attempt even bigger moves.

GRAB ON!

A grab is an aerial trick in which a rider reaches down and grabs hold of part of his or her board. Many types of grabs are performed in midair. A common grab is a **method grab**. To perform the method grab, a rider reaches back with his or her front hand to grab the heelside edge of the board. If the wakeboarder is riding in regular stance, then the rider's right hand is his or her front hand. If the wakeboarder is riding in goofy stance, then the rider's left hand is his or her front hand. Another well-known grab is called a **mute grab**. To perform the mute grab, the rider grabs the toeside edge of the board with his or her front hand. The rider above is performing a mute grab.

TAKE IT FOR A SPIN

A spin is a trick in which a rider turns himself or herself around, as shown right. A spin can be performed on the surface of the water or in midair. Spins are named for the number of times a rider turns. For example, a full spin is called a **360** because the rider turns around 360°. Some riders can even perform **1080s**. A 1080 is three full spins!

FLIPPED OUT!

A flip looks a lot like a midair cartwheel! To perform a flip, a rider cuts into a wake from the heelside. When the board pops up into the air, the rider swings his or her legs over his or her head before landing.

For many tricks, the rider must perform a handle pass to move the tow rope from one hand to the other while in midair.

WAKE TALK

Wakeboarders use terms and phrases from sports such as skateboarding to talk to one another about wakeboarding. The following are some of the common terms and phrases wakeboarders use.

boned: describes a move that is performed with great emphasis; to bone a leg during a trick means to straighten it as much as possible

bail: to leap clear of the board during a wipeout

glass: describes smooth, calm surface waters

choppy: describes rough surface waters

double-up: a powerboat crossing over its own wake, creating a double-sized wake for a rider to jump

getting slammed: wiping out while attempting a trick

sick: describes something that is really good or cool

throw down a move: to perform a trick

EXTREME EXPRESSION!

With practice and patience, wakeboarders learn to perform more extreme tricks. The pros train for countless hours to master these moves. Many extreme tricks are **combos**, or combinations of two or more tricks. In competitions, riders aim for the highest possible scores by performing the tricks **big**, or to the extreme. Riders receive high scores for performing the tricks shown on these pages because these tricks are considered more difficult than basic grabs, spins, and flips.

THE SKY'S THE LIMIT!

There are many combinations that riders can perform. Pro riders constantly challenge themselves to invent new combinations. Some combinations have unique names. One such combination is called the **roast beef**. To perform the roast beef, a rider passes her back hand through her legs and grabs the board on the heelside.

FLYING HIGH

During a **raley**, the rider seems to fly! She cuts into the wake on the heelside. Next, she straightens her arms and bends her knees, bringing the wakeboard high up in the air.

THROWING TANTRUMS!

Once riders can perform flips, they can try throwing **tantrums**! To perform tantrums, riders flip over backward instead of forward. They begin with their backs to the wakes and push their boards into the wakes. The riders are popped up, forcing their bodies into backward flips. They land facing the same way they started.

WAKEBOARDING COMPETITIONS

In wakeboarding competitions, competitors receive points based on the tricks they perform. Each competitor's ride consists of two passes along a course. First, the driver takes the rider through the course in one direction. Then the driver turns around and takes the rider through the course in the opposite direction. Each pass through a course lasts about 25 seconds.

Pros perform amazing tricks at competitions, such as this batwing.

BIGGER IS BETTER

As riders go through the course, they perform as many impressive aerial and surface tricks as they can. They try to go big on every trick to get the highest scores possible. The more extreme the tricks, the higher the scores are!

GO BIG OR GO HOME!

There are usually three judges scoring each competition. The judges sometimes ride in boats to make sure they have a clear view of the riders. The judges decide a rider's score based on how well they feel the rider performed each trick. A rider can receive a maximum combined score of 100 points from the judges. The judges do not count the first two times a wakeboarder falls. Riders lose points for each additional fall, however. In fact, many judges **disqualify** a rider if he or she falls three times.

BODY LANGUAGE

Riders use hand signals to communicate information to spotters. The World Wakeboard Association uses the following signals in its competitions:

rider gives a thumbs up: *he or she wants the driver to go faster*
rider gives a thumbs down: *he or she wants the driver to go slower*
rider points to a piece of equipment: *he or she has noticed a problem with the equipment*
rider points behind himself or herself: *he or she has spotted an object in the water*
rider raises a hand over his or her head: *he or she is requesting a* ***re-ride***

When riders wipe out, they must signal to let others know if they are okay. For example, if riders are hurt and want to be picked up, they may signal by tapping their heads.

Falling during a competition can end a rider's hopes of winning.

STAY THE COURSE

A wakeboarding competition course is planned by a **course designer**. A course designer creates courses that challenge the pros. When creating a course, the designer must follow the **regulations**, or standards, set out by the World Wakeboard Association. For example, the course must be between 1,200 and 1,500 feet (366 and 457 m) long. It should also have two bright orange **buoys**, or floating markers, indicating where the course begins and ends.

*A **slider** is an obstacle on which a rider slides his or her wakeboard. The rider moves along the entire length of the slider and then lands back on the water.*

22

KICK IT UP A NOTCH!

Most course designers add obstacles to their courses to increase the variety and difficulty of the tricks that can be performed. The obstacles may include **kickers**, sliders, and **slaughter boxes**. Riders that perform tricks using obstacles receive high scores.

Course designers must create obstacles that meet three main requirements for competitions—the obstacles must be safe, be well-made using specific materials, and be able to float and remain stable on water. Most obstacles are made using materials such as wood, metal, and a hard plastic called **PVC**.

A kicker is a ramp that sends a rider up into the air to perform tricks.

A slaughter box is an obstacle that looks like a slider and a kicker put together. Riders can slide along the edge or the top surface of a slaughter box.

X-TREME X-CITEMENT!

The most famous wakeboarding competition takes place each year at the Summer X Games. The X Games are extreme sports competitions that take place every summer and winter. The best extreme athletes from around the world compete in the X Games to win prizes, money, and medals. Wakeboarding became an X Games sport in 1996, when men's wakeboarding competitions were introduced. The women's competition was added a year later.

In 1996, Parks Bonifay won gold at the first X Games wakeboarding competition. He was only fourteen years old at the time!

DO YOU QUALIFY?

A few months before the X Games competition, an event is held to determine the top five male and the top three female wakeboarders. This qualifying event is known as an **X-trial**. Usually, only those riders who are successful during the X-trial are invited to compete in the X Games. More men than women are able to compete because there are currently many more male pro wakeboarders than there are female pro wakeboarders.

AUTOMATIC ADMISSION

Some wakeboarders qualify to compete in the X Games without taking part in the X-trial. For example, wakeboarders from the Asian X Games and from the Pro Wakeboard Tour automatically qualify to compete in the X Games.

The X Games have become one of the most popular extreme sports competitions in the world. The competitions showcase the amazing abilities of the world's top extreme athletes.

THE WINNERS' CIRCLE

Many pro wakeboarders became interested in their sport at an early age, when the sport was brand new. These stars have helped set the standard for excellence in wakeboarding. The taste of success has been sweet for some, earning them sponsorships from wakeboard manufacturers and clothing companies. Many companies even name their equipment after the world's top pro wakeboarders! Some of the famous young stars of wakeboarding are profiled here.

DALLAS FRIDAY

One of the most talented female pro wakeboarding stars is American Dallas Friday, shown above. Although she began her athletic career as a gymnast, Friday found that she excelled at a much different sport—wakeboarding! Her training as a gymnast gave her the confidence and ability to master complex tricks quickly. Friday has won many gold medals at the world's top competitions, including the X Games, World Cup, and Gravity Games.

TARA HAMILTON

In 1997, fifteen-year-old American wakeboarder Tara Hamilton entered the first women's X Games wakeboarding competition and took home the gold medal. She then went on to claim the Pro Wakeboarding Tour women's title, as well as the World Championship. This girl was awesome! Hamilton was at the top of her game when she injured her right heel in 2000. Many people believe it was her talent and dedication to wakeboarding that prompted other young female riders to burst onto the scene and take wakeboarding to a new level.

SHAUN MURRAY

American Shaun Murray has been wakeboarding since he was eleven years old. Nicknamed "The House of Style," Murray is widely known and respected for his smooth riding style and sick performances in competitions. He started competing in 1995 and has been a top-level performer on the pro circuit ever since. Murray's high level of ability and fun-loving attitude have caught the attention of wakeboarding fans around the world. In fact, he is even the star of a popular wakeboarding video game!

DARIN SHAPIRO

American Darin Shapiro is a wakeboarding legend. Shapiro began wakeboarding in 1991, at the age of 17. The following year, he became the World Tour champion, a title he held until 1996! Always going big and pushing the limits of the sport, Shapiro had an incredible year in 1998, when he claimed four pro titles: World Pro champion, Masters champion, X Games champion, and Sea World Big Air champion. Due to his success, he is famous all over the world. In Russia, there is even a competition named after him—the Shapiro Wake Cup!

PARKS BONIFAY

American Parks Bonifay, shown right, is known as the "Wonder Boy" of wakeboarding. He has participated in watersports all his life. At just six months old, he set a world record as the youngest water-skier ever! After winning gold at the X Games in 1996, Bonifay went on to become the first person to land a 1080 spin! This is still one of the most extreme wakeboarding moves ever performed. Bonifay continues to thrill audiences with his incredible abilities as he wins competitions all over the world.

SAFETY CHECK

Wakeboarding is an exciting sport, but it is also risky. Before any rider hits the water, there are many important safety checks he or she must perform. Every rider must also gear up in the proper equiment. A good rider is a safe rider!

GETTING STARTED

Before every ride, the rider and boat driver must check the powerboat carefully to ensure that everything is running properly. The rider, driver, and spotter then review the signals they will use to communicate while on the water. The boat driver should also be aware of the rider's skill level. Drivers go at slower speeds for beginners, to allow them better control over their wakeboards.

Wakeboards should never be used in shallow water or near shores, docks, swimmers, or other boats and riders.

GET A HANDLE ON IT

It is important that riders inspect their tow ropes and handles carefully each time they wakeboard. Frayed or damaged ropes could break during rides. Chips or cracks in the handles could also cause injuries to the hands of riders during tricks and handle passes.

THE RIGHT FIT

A professional at a wakeboard shop should fit each rider's board and bindings. Bindings must be properly secured to the board and be snug on each foot. However, if a wipeout does occur, the rider's feet should release fairly easily to help him or her avoid injuries.

The pros always use high-quality gear, and they inspect it carefully before every ride to keep themselves and others safe.

GET ON BOARD!

Wakeboarding is a great sport for people who love to be challenged. Do you feel like giving it a whirl? It requires patience and determination to master the basics of wakeboarding before attempting more advanced moves. Remember that the tricks you see in this book are performed by experienced professionals—not beginners. Learning to wakeboard is a long process! It will take time to get comfortable, so set goals and stick to them. For beginners who are eager to improve their skills, wakeboarding camps, instructional videos, and websites offer plenty of information about the sport.

NO BOAT? NO PROBLEM!

People who do not have access to a powerboat can try wakeboarding at **cable wakeboarding parks**. In these parks, wakeboarders hold onto tow ropes and are pulled around square-shaped waterways. The tow ropes are attached to cables. The cables are 24 to 39 feet (7-12 m) above the surface of the water. They are held up by a set of four or five towers. The tow ropes are powered by electric motors that can operate at different speeds.

MANY BENEFITS

There are currently fewer than 100 cable wakeboarding parks in the world, but they are quickly gaining in popularity. There is no limit to how many times a rider can go around the waterway, so a park is a great place to practice without worrying about a powerboat running out of gas! Going to a cable wakeboarding park is a safe and affordable way for beginners to learn how to wakeboard, so get out there and go big!

GLOSSARY

Note: Boldfaced words that are defined in the text may not appear in the glossary.

course A mapped-out area in which wakeboarders ride during competitions

binding Equipment that attaches a rider's feet to a wakeboard

disqualify To force an athlete to leave a competition

fiberglass A material made from very fine pieces of glass

graphite A very fine powder used to create a top coat for some wakeboards

handle pass A trick in which a rider passes the handle from one hand to the other

obstacle An object that is in the way

powerboat A boat that is powered by an engine

recreational Describes an activity that is performed for fun

re-ride A second attempt at a ride during a competition; a re-ride can be granted only by a judge and is granted only for equipment or boat failure or due to a driver's error

snowboard A board that is used to ride down snow-covered hills

surfboard A long board made of hard foam and fiberglass that is used to ride ocean waves

tow rope A rope that a wakeboarder holds as he or she is pulled by a powerboat

twin-tip wakeboard A wakeboard that is rounded at both ends

X Games A series of extreme sports events

INDEX

1 2 3 4 5 6 7 8 9 0 Printed in the U.S.A. 5 4 3 2 1 0 9 8 7 6